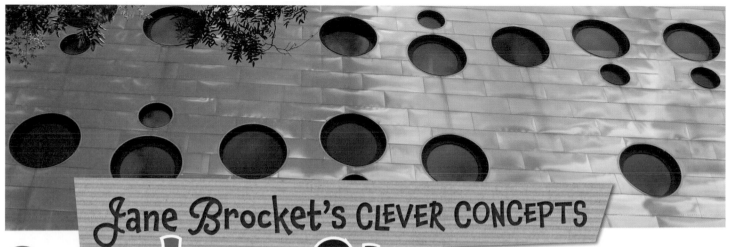

*Jane Brocket's* CLEVER CONCEPTS

# Circles, Stars, and Squares

## Looking for SHAPES

M

Millbrook Press • Minneapolis

Take a look at this book.
Do you know what shape it is?
Every object has a shape, and
the world is full of interesting
SHAPES.

Let's see what shapes we can find.

You can draw and paint **flat shapes** on paper.

4

**Solid shapes** are different. You can make them with your hands using clay or dough or bricks.

A **circle** is flat and round and curving. It doesn't have any straight lines or sharp edges, like these stickers and the holes in this cake carrier.

An **oval** is a circle that has been squashed
in the middle, like this window.

A **square** has four straight sides all the same, with four sharp corners all the same. Squares are regular and even.

A **rectangle** also has four sides,
but two are long and two are short.

Rectangles can be found in many places. Bricks, doors, and windows are rectangles we see every day.

Which shape has three
sides and three corners?

12

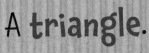

A **triangle**.
Some triangles have sides that are all the same length. Some have sides of different lengths.

13

Two triangles together can make a **diamond**. A diamond has four equal sides and two very sharp points. We can see diamonds in fishing nets, quilts, and windows.

Flat shapes with more than four sides have their own special names. A **pentagon** has five sides.

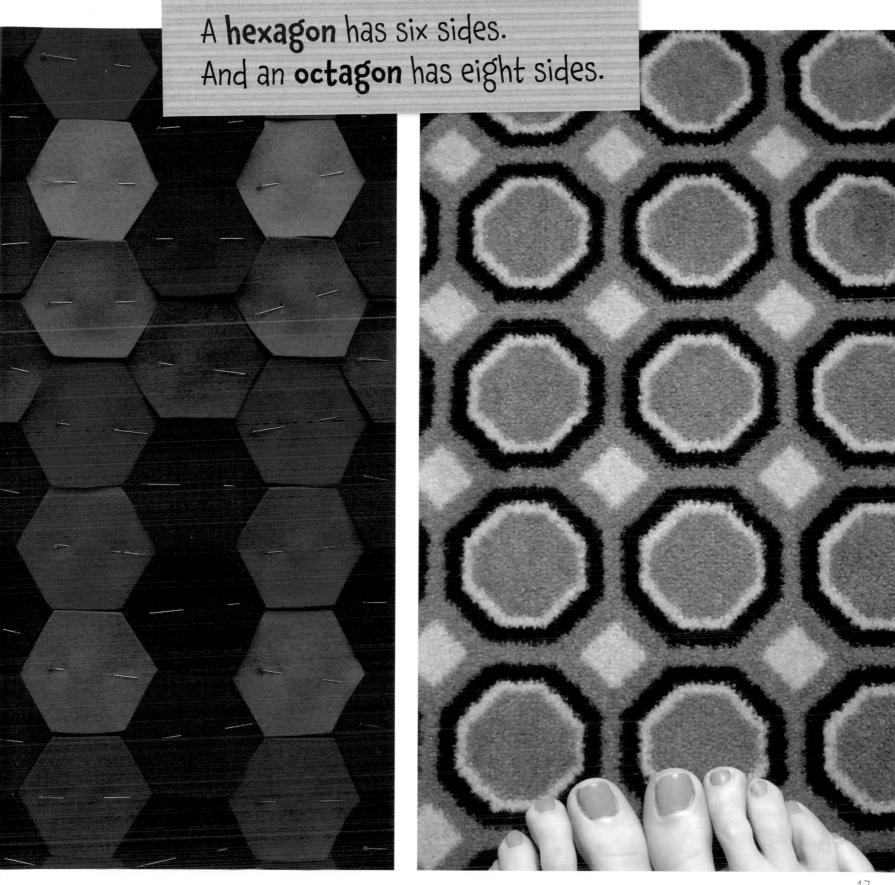

A **hexagon** has six sides.
And an **octagon** has eight sides.

So far, we have found **flat shapes**, so now let's take a look at **solid shapes**.

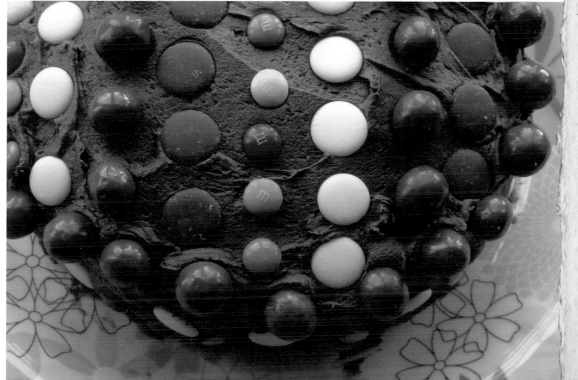

A solid circle is called a **sphere**. Tomatoes, balls of yarn, oranges, and chocolate candies are all spheres.

A **cylinder** has circles at each end and straight sides in between.

Cylinders are useful shapes
for buildings . . .

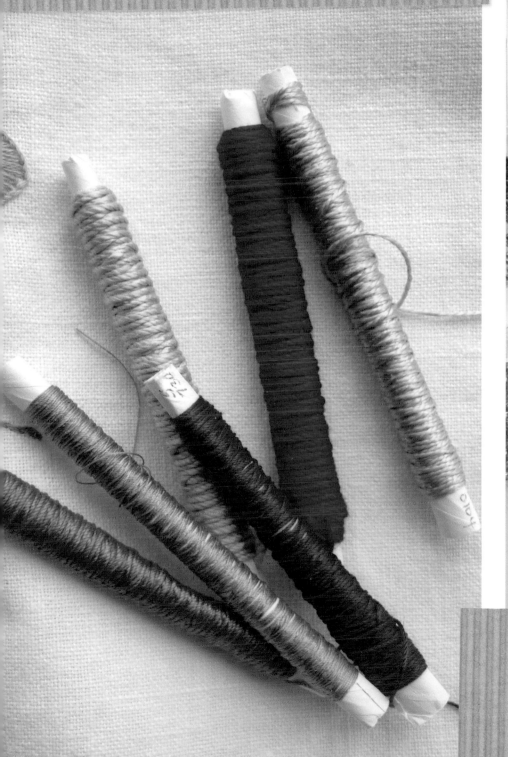

and for keeping threads
and tiny beads tidy.

A **cube** is a solid square with flat surfaces.
Can you count how many equal sides,
edges, and corners a cube has?*

Sweet candy and iced cakes can be shaped like cubes, and even little play figures can get stuck in plastic cubes!

**Cones** have a point at one end and a circle at the other. Sometimes they are solid, like this sculpture. Sometimes they are hollow, like these paper cones. Cones are also useful for holding treats!

Some shapes look like other shapes but are a little different.

**Rings** are circles with the middle taken out. Bright red life jackets, sugar cookies, and shiny metal door knockers are all rings.

Eggs are almost ovals, but they have one pointier end and one rounder end.

A **heart** can make us feel happy.
Sweet heart-shaped cakes make us smile.

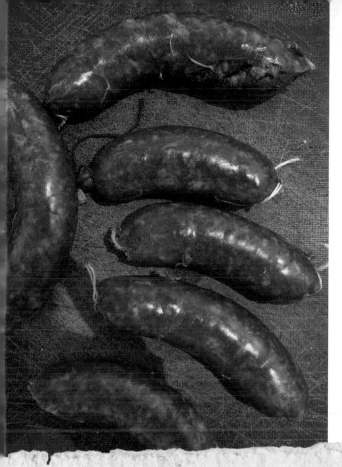

Some shapes don't have their own names, so we say they look like something else. An object can be **sausage-shaped** or **pear-shaped** or **star-shaped**.

And pasta shapes include **shells**, **curly wiggles, pointy tubes, and bow ties.**

We have found lots of interesting shapes.
Now, take a look around you.
Can you name the **SHAPES** you see?

Millbrook Press
A division of Lerner Publishing Group, Inc.
241 First Avenue North
Minneapolis, MN 55401 U.S.A.

Website address: www.lernerbooks.com


Main body text set in Chaloops Regular 24/32.
Typeface provided by Chank.

Library of Congress Cataloging-in-Publication Data

Brocket, Jane.
    Circles, stars, and squares : looking for shapes / by Jane Brocket ;
  photographs by Jane Brocket.
      p.   cm. — (Jane Brocket's clever concepts)
    ISBN 978—0—7613—4611—1 (lib. bdg. : alk. paper)
    1. Shapes—Juvenile literature.  2. Geometry, Plane—Juvenile literature.
    I. Title.
    QA445.5.B75  2013
    516'.15—dc23                                   2011050199

Manufactured in the United States of America
1 — DP — 7/15/12

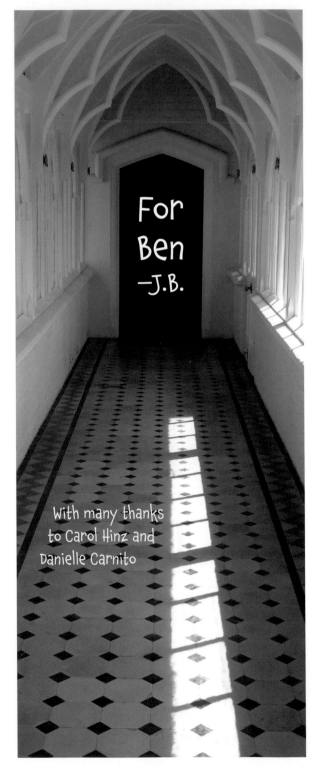

For
Ben
—J.B.

With many thanks
to Carol Hinz and
Danielle Carnito